CONTENTS

D1372028

ANSEL ADAMS (1902–1984)

One of America's best-known photographers, Ansel Adams used large, heavy cameras to make extraordinary images. He loved the outdoors, and many of his pictures captured the beauty of the mountains and the desert. Adams was a member of the Sierra Club, which works to preserve America's natural resources.

AMERICAN
HEROES

COLORING BOOK

STEVEN JAMES PETRUCCIO

DOVER PUBLICATIONS, INC.
MINEOLA, NEW YORK

Bibliographical Note

American Heroes Coloring Book is a new work, first published by
Dover Publications, Inc., in 2013.

International Standard Book Number

ISBN-13: 978-0-486-49895-9
ISBN-10: 0-486-49895-6

Manufactured in the United States by LSC Communications
49895603   2019
www.doverpublications.com

NOTE

From the American past to the American present, this inspiring book contains ready-to-color images of great figures in science, social activism, sports, technology, law, politics, the arts, and American history itself. As you read the biographies you'll discover the many forms that heroism can take. Enjoy coloring the images of these forty-three men and women whose courage, talent, and genius have contributed to the greatness of the country and enriched the lives of all Americans.

JANE ADDAMS (1860–1935)

Jane Addams dedicated herself to helping poor Americans live better lives. She and a friend bought a big house in Chicago, which they named Hull House, and opened it to needy families in the area. Here they founded a kindergarten, a gym, and a playground. Addams devoted herself to social causes such as ending child labor.

SUSAN B. ANTHONY (1820–1906)

Susan B. Anthony, an educated woman and teacher, supported the right of women to vote. She worked toward the passage of an amendment to give American women that right (the Nineteenth Amendment to the Constitution passed in 1920). Anthony also supported the antislavery movement.

NEIL ARMSTRONG (1930–2012)

On July 20, 1969, NASA astronaut Neil Armstrong became the first person to walk on the moon. When he looked down at his own footprint on the surface of the moon, he uttered the famous words "That's one small step for [a] man, one giant leap for mankind."

CLARA BARTON (1821–1912)

After opening a free school in New Jersey, Clara Barton moved to Washington, D.C., to work in the U.S. Patent Office. However, women were not favored for government work, and Barton lost her job. During the Civil War, she was active in sending medical and other supplies to the soldiers. One of her best-known achievements is the founding of the American Red Cross.

ALEXANDER GRAHAM BELL (1847–1922)

Alexander Graham Bell is best-known as the inventor of the telephone, for which he received a U.S. patent in 1876. After moving with his family from his native Scotland to Canada, Bell opened a school that had many deaf pupils (his mother and wife were deaf, which influenced his research), one of whom was Helen Keller. Bell later moved to the United States, where he served as president of the National Geographic Society.

DANIEL BOONE (1734–1820)

In the 1700s, the western lands of America, home to Native Americans, were largely unknown to the settlers in the East. Daniel Boone, who was born in Pennsylvania and grew up in North Carolina, led dangerous exploratory expeditions to the West. His Wilderness Trail was used by thousands of western-bound settlers. He brought his family with him on one trip, founding Boonesboro in Kentucky. Daniel Boone's courage and spirit of adventure opened up the western frontier for settlement.

RICHARD BYRD (1888–1957)

After receiving an education at U.S. military schools, Richard Byrd became a naval officer and aviator. In 1926, Byrd, the navigator, and Floyd Bennett, the pilot, made what they claimed was the first flight over the North Pole (some doubted their claim). Byrd and Bennett received the U.S. Congressional Medal of Honor. Byrd later explored Antarctica and also contributed to the knowledge of navigating over water while out of sight of land.

CESAR CHAVEZ (1927–1993)

Born into a family that moved from place to place in search of farm work, Cesar Chavez knew firsthand the long hours, low pay, and difficult work of the migrant farmer. When he was older, he helped get farm workers to form a union, and, in 1965, he led unions to strike against some of the companies that grew grapes in California. His efforts helped farm workers live better lives.

FREDERICK DOUGLASS (1817[?]–1895)

Douglass, the son of a slave, saw education as the way to promote the movement to end slavery in the U.S. He became a well-known speaker against slavery, founded a newspaper, helped run the Underground Railroad, and was the U.S. minister to Haiti when in his seventies.

AMELIA EARHART (1897–1937)

In her short life, Amelia Earhart achieved many things: she worked as a nurse during WWI and as a social worker in Boston, but her greatest fame came from her piloting a plane alone across the Atlantic Ocean—and in record time! She also made the first solo flight across the Pacific. Sadly, she and her navigator disappeared during an attempt to fly around the world in 1937.

THOMAS A. EDISON (1847–1931)

One of America's greatest inventors, Thomas Edison is associated with the phonograph (which he called a "talking machine") and the electric light bulb. He also contributed to the development of the telephone, which was invented by Alexander Graham Bell. His "Black Maria," founded in 1893, was the first film studio, where he made the first motion picture.

ALBERT EINSTEIN (1879–1955)

Albert Einstein was a brilliant scientist and mathematician whose discoveries have had a lasting impact. He and his family came to the United States from Germany in the early 1930s to escape religious persecution, and Einstein continued his career at Princeton University in New Jersey. After some of his discoveries were used to develop atomic bombs, he turned his attention to finding ways to achieve world peace (which had interested him for some time).

HENRY FORD (1863–1947)

The founder of the Ford Motor Company, Henry Ford wanted to sell cars to average Americans— not just the wealthy, who were the only ones who could afford them. Ford developed ways to bring down the price of cars, such as using an assembly line (workers added parts in a particular order as the car bodies moved along the "line," rather than having a single person or a team make one car). Ford also paid his workers more than the average wage, enabling them to live better and buy more, which was good for the economy.

BENJAMIN FRANKLIN (1706–1790)

Born in Boston, Benjamin Franklin traveled to Philadelphia and then London, but returned to Philadelphia, where he printed a newspaper, founded what later became the University of Pennsylvania, helped draft the Declaration of Independence during the American Revolution, and signed a petition to Congress to end slavery. His invention of the lightning rod came out of an experiment with a kite to which he had attached a key.

BILL GATES (b. 1955)

One of the most successful businesspeople in the world, and a leader in the field of computer technology, Bill Gates followed his interest in writing computer programs to start a computer software company with Paul Allen at Harvard University. Through the development of the Microsoft operating system for the growing market for personal computers, Gates became tremendously successful. He has used his great personal wealth to invest in developing areas such as Africa.

THOMAS JEFFERSON (1743–1826)

In addition to serving as America's third president, Thomas Jefferson was a writer—he wrote the first draft of the Declaration of Independence—as well as a diplomat, an architect, and a farmer. In addition, he practiced law, was minister to France (after Ben Franklin), and wrote the Virginia Statute of Religious Freedom during his time as governor of the state.

STEVE JOBS (1955–2011)

Like Bill Gates, Steve Jobs has transformed the way people live through technology. Growing up in the 1950s in an area of California that was rapidly developing new fields of electronics, Jobs became involved with other young people who were making computers and writing software programs. He and a friend, Stephen Wozniak, founded Apple Computer in 1976. In 1981, Jobs became head of the Macintosh division of Apple, and his later projects, such as the iPod, the iPad, and the iPhone, became huge hits with electronics consumers around the world.

JOHN PAUL JONES (1747–1792)

A native of Scotland, Jones fought on the side of America during the Revolutionary War and achieved many victories against the British. His daring maneuvers, especially a 1779 defeat of Britain during a naval attack, led to his being hailed as a hero. He received a Congressional gold medal in 1787 for his dedication to the American cause.

CHIEF JOSEPH (1840–1904)

A member of the Nez Perce in the Pacific Northwest region, Chief Joseph was recognized for his leadership during a period when the U.S. government was removing Native Americans from their lands and relocating them to smaller "reservations." In 1877, he led the Nez Perce on a journey of more than 1,000 miles, with the U.S. Army in pursuit. Chief Joseph surrendered, but two years later, he went to Washington, D.C., to meet with President Hayes, and he was permitted to return with his followers to the Pacific Northwest.

HELEN KELLER & ANNE SULLIVAN (1880–1968; 1866–1936)

After a childhood illness left her deaf, blind, and unable to speak, Helen Keller was cut off from the world around her. With her teacher, Anne Sullivan (recommended by Alexander Graham Bell), Helen discovered that things had names.

This was the beginning of her connection with the world, as Anne Sullivan patiently taught Helen ways to learn and communicate, including Braille and sign language. She went to college and wrote a book, *The Story of My Life* (1903).

BILLIE JEAN KING (b. 1943)

As a child growing up in California, Billie Jean Moffitt (later Billie Jean King, after she married), discovered her talent as a tennis player. She began winning tournaments and was ranked No. 1 in the world in the mid-1960s. Women's tennis was not taken as seriously as men's at the time, and when Billie Jean King discovered that male tennis players won more prize money than female players, she began a fight for equality. In 1973, King won a nationally televised match against male player Bobby Riggs.

She received a 2009 Presidential Medal of Freedom.

MARTIN LUTHER KING JR. (1929–1968)

It is hard to overestimate the influence that Martin Luther King Jr. has had on the fight for civil rights both in America and around the world. He dedicated himself to fighting for freedom and justice using non-violent means, as the Indian leader Mahatma Gandhi had done. In an attempt to do away with laws that discriminated against African Americans, Dr. King led the March on Washington for Jobs and Freedom in Washington, D.C., in 1963. A year later, the Civil Rights Act was passed. Dr. King, who won the Nobel Peace Prize, was assassinated in 1968.

MAGGIE KUHN (1905–1995)

A turning point in Maggie Kuhn's life came at the age of sixty-five, when she was required to retire from her job. This event marked the beginning of her crusade against what many saw as age discrimination. Along with some friends, Maggie Kuhn founded the Gray Panthers, a group whose goal was to change people's minds about the abilities of older adults, as well as protecting them with laws. Her activism inspired people to view growing older in new ways.

LEWIS & CLARK (1774–1809; 1770–1838) AND SACAJAWEA (c. 1787–1812[?])

The story of the exploration of the American West would not be complete without Lewis and Clark, as well as Sacajawea. President Thomas Jefferson asked Meriwether Lewis and William Clark to lead an expedition through the Louisiana Territory in 1804, with the goal of exploring the land and finding a way to reach the Pacific Coast by water. Sacajawea, an excellent guide, helped them find their way and found horses for their difficult travel. The expedition reached the Pacific Ocean in 1805.

JOHN MUIR (1838–1914)

The environmental movement owes much to the efforts of John Muir. After moving with his family to America from his native Scotland, Muir traveled around the country, often on foot. He developed an intense love of nature and began to write articles that made him famous. National Parks such as Yosemite were created due to his effort to protect "wild" lands, and Muir was a founder of the Sierra Club, an environmental organization.

AUDIE MURPHY (1925–1971)

Audie Murphy signed up to fight in Europe during World War II. His bravery during combat led to his receiving the highest military award of the United States, the Medal of Honor. This award recognizes that the person being honored has gone "above and beyond the call of duty." He was nineteen when he received it. After the war, Audie Murphy turned to show business, appearing in more than forty Hollywood movies, including one based on his book about his war experiences.

SANDRA DAY O'CONNOR (b. 1930)

Although Sandra Day O'Connor performed exceptionally well in law school, she had difficulty being hired as an attorney because of prejudices against women. She worked for the government and became active in politics. Sandra Day O'Connor's career is distinguished by these "firsts": First Republican Majority Leader in the Arizona State Senate (1972), and later, the first female Supreme Court Justice (1981). She fought against discrimination against women in various areas, including the field of law itself.

JESSE OWENS (1913–1980)

Jesse Owens began running and competing in track events as a student and gained national attention as a student athlete at Ohio State University. The world learned of his athletic abilities when Owens competed at the 1936 Olympic Games in Berlin, Germany. Adolf Hitler, the Nazi leader, intended to use the Games to demonstrate his belief in the superiority of the Germanic race. Jesse Owens won four gold medals and set and tied world records at the Games, showing the world the great achievements of this African American athlete.

SALLY RIDE (1951–2012)

Growing up, Sally Ride was a gifted athlete. However, her love of science led her to study physics as well as astronomy. She was one of only five women who applied to train to become an astronaut at NASA (there were eight thousand applicants). Sally Ride became the first American woman in space when she orbited Earth in the space shuttle *Challenger* in 1983. After her experiences as an astronaut, she turned to teaching, and she spent much of her time encouraging girls to study science.

JACKIE ROBINSON (1919–1972)

Before Jackie Robinson, African Americans were barred from playing baseball in the major leagues—there were separate Negro Leagues. Robinson, a great student athlete, was chosen by Branch Rickey, the president of the Brooklyn Dodgers, to play on the team. Although many players treated Robinson poorly, he was determined to take his place as the first African American to play Major League baseball. Many more African Americans were hired in baseball, as well as other professional sports.

ELEANOR ROOSEVELT (1884–1962)

Eleanor Roosevelt was married to the thirty-second American president, Franklin Delano Roosevelt. As First Lady, she became an active political partner to her husband, who had polio. The First Lady traveled around the country to see the effects of the programs that Roosevelt had developed to benefit Americans. She also devoted herself to expanding the rights of women and minorities in the U.S. Her many newspaper and magazine articles and speeches made her a well-known figure for social change.

JONAS SALK (1914–1995)

Polio, an infectious disease that can lead to paralysis, was feared for many years. President Franklin Roosevelt lost the use of his legs after being stricken with polio. Jonas Salk, a medical researcher, began working with a team to study the polio virus, with the goal of developing a vaccine. The testers of the vaccine included hundreds of thousands of doctors, school children, and volunteers.

SEQUOYA (c. 1770–1843)

As settlers moved across America in search of new homes, the native population felt threatened. A leader of the Cherokee Nation, Sequoya, wanted to help the Cherokee keep their land and maintain their way of life. Sequoya, a hunter, fur trader, and silversmith, believed that by teaching the Native Americans to read and write, he could help them maintain their way of life. He devoted himself to creating a Cherokee alphabet and language to be used by the Cherokee Nation.

NIKOLA TESLA (1856–1943)

Nikola Tesla, a Serb born in what is today Croatia, came to the United States in 1884. With a background in electronics and experience working at a telephone company in Hungary, Tesla was hired by Thomas Edison. After redesigning some of Edison's equipment (with little financial reward), Tesla founded his own company, Tesla Electric Light & Manufacturing. He is famous for his development of AC (alternating current) electric power used by businesses and homes, as well as radio control and wireless communication.

SOJOURNER TRUTH (c. 1797–1883)

Sojourner Truth, born Isabella Baumfree, was the daughter of African slaves who lived in New York. Truth, bought and sold a number of times, escaped with a daughter but left behind her other children. She went to court to recover her son, a slave in Alabama, and became the first African American to win a court case against a white man. She is known for the speeches she gave against slavery, as well as for her support of women's rights.

NOAH WEBSTER (1758–1843)

While employed as a teacher, Noah Webster decided that American children should use textbooks made in America, rather than those produced in England. He wrote the "Blue-Backed Speller," which sold millions of copies and was used in classrooms by a vast number of American schoolchildren. This American writer and educator, however, is best known for his dictionary, which he first published in 1806. His efforts to create a distinctly American language eliminated many English spellings (such as *colour* for *color* and *centre* for *center*).

ORVILLE & WILBUR WRIGHT (1871–1948; 1867–1912)

The Wright brothers became interested in building flying machines after designing toys, making a printing press, and founding a bicycle business featuring their own brand. Orville and Wilbur built and tested several gliders, but it wasn't until they built a plane with a gas-powered engine that they began to get recognition for their efforts. On December 17, 1903, at Kitty Hawk, North Carolina, the brothers succeeded in keeping their plane, the Wright Flyer, in the air for twelve seconds—powered flight had begun!

CHUCK YEAGER (b. 1923)

From his experiences as a fighter pilot during World War II, to his years as a U.S. test pilot, Charles "Chuck" Yeager has been a courageous pioneer. In 1947, he volunteered to test an experimental plane, and went on to break the sound barrier later in that year—speeding through the sky at 662 miles per hour! He also achieved a world record for speed, piloting an aircraft with rocket power at 1,650 miles per hour in 1953. Yeager continued to do test flights into the 1990s.

INDEX